100

THINGS TO DO AFTER I GRADUATE

My Bucket List of Adventures

PAPER PANDA
PRESS

Gentle Reminders:

 Visit this journal every morning. Keep your eyes on the goal at the start of the day.

 Start with simple goals that are quick to accomplish:

> *Try new dishes to savor and prepare*
> *Practice self-love, meditation, gratitude*
> *Learn new things (music, sports, art)*
> *Travel and explore new places*
> *Help others, share your time & blessings*

 Scan pages 109 to 112 and be inspired by 100 epic and funny bucket list ideas

 Deep breaths. Take your time. Have fun doing this!

 Shade 5 stars if it was unforgettable!

Check the box once the "deed" is done. Then, give yourself a pat on the back.

ISBN-13: 979-8618355551

Email us! paperpandapress@gmail.com

Your life is an
expression of
all your thoughts.

Marcus Aurelius

THIS BUCKET LIST BELONGS TO

_____

_____

_____

_____

Let the Adventure Begin!

- [ ] 1.
- [ ] 2.
- [ ] 3.
- [ ] 4.
- [ ] 5.
- [ ] 6.
- [ ] 7.
- [ ] 8.
- [ ] 9.
- [ ] 10.
- [ ] 11.
- [ ] 12.
- [ ] 13.
- [ ] 14.
- [ ] 15.
- [ ] 16.
- [ ] 17.
- [ ] 18.
- [ ] 19.
- [ ] 20.
- [ ] 21.
- [ ] 22.

Keep It Coming...

- [ ] 23.
- [ ] 24.
- [ ] 25.
- [ ] 26.
- [ ] 27.
- [ ] 28.
- [ ] 29.
- [ ] 30.
- [ ] 31.
- [ ] 32.
- [ ] 33.
- [ ] 34.
- [ ] 35.
- [ ] 36.
- [ ] 37.
- [ ] 38.
- [ ] 39.
- [ ] 40.
- [ ] 41.
- [ ] 42.
- [ ] 43.
- [ ] 44.

Just Warming Up..

☐ 45.

☐ 46.

☐ 47.

☐ 48.

☐ 49.

☐ 50.

☐ 51.

☐ 52.

☐ 53.

☐ 54.

☐ 55.

☐ 56.

☐ 57.

☐ 58.

☐ 59.

☐ 60.

☐ 61.

☐ 62.

☐ 63.

☐ 64.

☐ 65.

☐ 66.

Happy Days Ahead!

- [ ] 67.
- [ ] 68.
- [ ] 69.
- [ ] 70.
- [ ] 71.
- [ ] 72.
- [ ] 73.
- [ ] 74.
- [ ] 75.
- [ ] 76.
- [ ] 77.
- [ ] 78.
- [ ] 79.
- [ ] 80.
- [ ] 81.
- [ ] 82.
- [ ] 83.
- [ ] 84.
- [ ] 85.
- [ ] 86.
- [ ] 87.
- [ ] 88.

Adventure Never Ends...

89.

90.

91.

92.

93.

94.

95.

96.

97.

98.

99.

100.

▶ _____

1

WHY I want to do this ~

Things I **NEED** ~

Ready, steady... ➚ *GO!!!* _____ DATE ACCOMPLISHED

My Experience ~ ☆ ☆ ☆ ☆ ☆

Awesome learnings & MEMORIES to keep ~

"Life shrinks or expands in proportion
to one's courage."

~ Anais Nin

2 ▶ _____

_____

WHY I want to do this ~

Things I **NEED** ~

DATE ACCOMPLISHED · _Ready, steady..._ ➚ _GO!!!_

My Experience ~ ☆ ☆ ☆ ☆ ☆

Awesome learnings & MEMORIES to keep ~

▶ _____

3

_____

WHY I want to do this ~

Things I **NEED** ~

Ready, steady... 🏹 *GO!!!* _____
DATE ACCOMPLISHED

My Experience ~ ☆ ☆ ☆ ☆ ☆

Awesome learnings & MEMORIES to keep ~

"Change happens for you the moment you want
something more than you fear it."

~ Eric Micha'el Leventhal

4

_____

_____

WHY I want to do this ~

_____

Things I **NEED** ~

_____

_____ DATE ACCOMPLISHED *Ready, steady...* ➔ *GO!!!*

My Experience ~ ☆ ☆ ☆ ☆ ☆

Awesome learnings & MEMORIES to keep ~

_____

_____

_____

_____

_____

_____

_____

_____

_____

_____

▶ _____

5

_____

WHY I want to do this ~
_____

Things I **NEED** ~
_____

Ready, steady... 🏹 *GO!!!* _____

My Experience ~ ☆ ☆ ☆ ☆ ☆
_____

Awesome learnings & MEMORIES to keep ~
_____
_____
_____
_____
_____
_____
_____
_____
_____

"Experience is the teacher of all things."

~ Julius Caesar

6 ▶ _____

WHY I want to do this ~

Things I **NEED** ~

DATE ACCOMPLISHED ____ *Ready, steady...* ➔ *GO!!!*

My Experience ~ ☆☆☆☆☆

Awesome learnings & MEMORIES to keep ~

▶ _____

7

_____

WHY I want to do this ~

_____

Things I **NEED** ~

_____

Ready, steady... 🔥 **GO!!!** _____
DATE ACCOMPLISHED

My Experience ~ ☆ ☆ ☆ ☆ ☆

Awesome learnings & MEMORIES to keep ~

_____

_____

_____

_____

_____

_____

_____

_____

"Defeat is always momentary."

~ Carl Denham (King Kong 2005)

8 ▶ _____

WHY I want to do this ~

Things I **NEED** ~

_____ *Ready, steady...* ✈ *GO!!!*
DATE ACCOMPLISHED

My Experience ~ ☆ ☆ ☆ ☆ ☆

Awesome learnings & MEMORIES to keep ~

▶ _____

9

_____

WHY I want to do this ~

Things I **NEED** ~

Ready, steady... ♂ *GO!!!* _____
DATE ACCOMPLISHED

My Experience ~ ☆ ☆ ☆ ☆ ☆

Awesome learnings & MEMORIES to keep ~

"Every 'no' is a 'yes' to something."

~ Eric Micha'el Leventhal

10

_____

_____

WHY I want to do this ~

_____

Things I **NEED** ~

_____

_____ DATE ACCOMPLISHED _____ *Ready, steady...* **GO!!!**

My Experience ~ ☆ ☆ ☆ ☆ ☆

Awesome learnings & MEMORIES to keep ~

▶ _____

11

_____

WHY I want to do this ~
_____

Things I **NEED** ~
_____

Ready, steady... 🖊 **GO!!!** _____
DATE ACCOMPLISHED

My Experience ~ ☆ ☆ ☆ ☆ ☆
_____

Awesome learnings & MEMORIES to keep ~
_____
_____
_____
_____
_____
_____
_____
_____

"A man's true wealth is the good he does in the world."

~ Khalil Gibran

12

_____

_____

WHY I want to do this ~

_____

_____

Things I **NEED** ~

_____

_____

———— DATE ACCOMPLISHED ———— _Ready, steady..._ ➤ **GO!!!**

My Experience ~ ☆ ☆ ☆ ☆ ☆

Awesome learnings & MEMORIES to keep ~

_____

_____

_____

_____

_____

_____

_____

_____

_____

_____

_____

_____

▶ _____

13

_____

WHY I want to do this ~

_____

Things I **NEED** ~

_____

Ready, steady... 🎯 *GO!!!* _____

DATE ACCOMPLISHED

My Experience ~ ☆ ☆ ☆ ☆ ☆

_____

Awesome learnings & MEMORIES to keep ~

_____

_____

_____

_____

_____

_____

_____

_____

"Live as if you were to die tomorrow,
learn as if you were to live forever."

~ Mahatma Gandhi

14 ▶ _____

_____

_____

WHY I want to do this ~

_____

Things I **NEED** ~

_____

_____ Ready, steady... ↗ GO!!!
DATE ACCOMPLISHED

My Experience ~ ☆ ☆ ☆ ☆ ☆

Awesome learnings & MEMORIES to keep ~

_____

_____

_____

_____

_____

_____

_____

_____

_____

_____

▶ _____

15

_____

WHY I want to do this ~

Things I **NEED** ~

Ready, steady... ➔ *GO!!!* _____
DATE ACCOMPLISHED

My Experience ~ ☆ ☆ ☆ ☆ ☆

Awesome learnings & MEMORIES to keep ~

"It does not matter how slowly you go
as long as you do not stop."

~ Confucius

16

_____

WHY I want to do this ~

Things I **NEED** ~

_____ DATE ACCOMPLISHED _____ *Ready, steady...* **GO!!!**

My Experience ~ ☆☆☆☆☆

Awesome learnings & MEMORIES to keep ~

▶ _____

_____

17

WHY I want to do this ~
_____

Things I **NEED** ~
_____

Ready, steady... ➷ **GO!!!** _____
DATE ACCOMPLISHED

My Experience ~ ☆ ☆ ☆ ☆ ☆
_____

Awesome learnings & MEMORIES to keep ~

_____

_____

_____

_____

_____

_____

_____

_____

"Ask for what you want and be prepared to get it!"

~ Maya Angelou

18 ▶ _____

_____

WHY I want to do this ~

_____

Things I **NEED** ~

_____

_____ DATE ACCOMPLISHED   *Ready, steady...* 🏁 *GO!!!*

My Experience ~ ☆ ☆ ☆ ☆ ☆

Awesome learnings & MEMORIES to keep ~

▶ _____

_____

19

WHY I want to do this ~

Things I **NEED** ~

Ready, steady... ↗ *GO!!!* _____
DATE ACCOMPLISHED

My Experience ~ ☆ ☆ ☆ ☆ ☆

Awesome learnings & MEMORIES to keep ~

"Begin to live as though your prayers
are already answered."

~ Tony Robbins

20 ▶ _____

_____

_____

WHY I want to do this ~

Things I **NEED** ~

_____ *Ready, steady...* 🏹 *GO!!!*
DATE ACCOMPLISHED

My Experience ~ ☆ ☆ ☆ ☆ ☆

Awesome learnings & MEMORIES to keep ~

▶ _____

21

_____

WHY I want to do this ~

Things I **NEED** ~

Ready, steady... ➫ *GO!!!* _____
DATE ACCOMPLISHED

My Experience ~ ☆ ☆ ☆ ☆ ☆

Awesome learnings & MEMORIES to keep ~

"If you see it in your mind. You'll hold it in your hand."

~ Bob Proctor

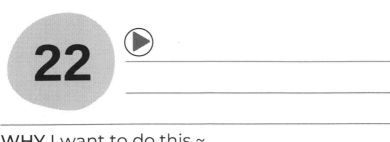

22 ▶ _____

_____

WHY I want to do this ~

_____

Things I **NEED** ~

_____

_____ DATE ACCOMPLISHED _____ *Ready, steady...* ✈ *GO!!!*

My Experience ~ ☆☆☆☆☆

Awesome learnings & MEMORIES to keep ~

▶ _____

23

_____

WHY I want to do this ~

Things I **NEED** ~

Ready, steady... 🏃 **GO!!!** _____
DATE ACCOMPLISHED

My Experience ~ ☆ ☆ ☆ ☆ ☆

Awesome learnings & MEMORIES to keep ~

"We are what we repeatedly do.
Excellence, then, is not an act, but a habit."

~ Aristotle

24 ▶ _____

_____

WHY I want to do this ~
_____

Things I **NEED** ~
_____

DATE ACCOMPLISHED — *Ready, steady...* ➤ *GO!!!*

My Experience ~ ☆ ☆ ☆ ☆ ☆

Awesome learnings & MEMORIES to keep ~

_____
_____
_____
_____
_____
_____
_____
_____
_____
_____
_____
_____

25

_____

_____

WHY I want to do this ~

Things I **NEED** ~

Ready, steady... 🏇 **GO!!!** _____
DATE ACCOMPLISHED

My Experience ~ ☆ ☆ ☆ ☆ ☆

Awesome learnings & MEMORIES to keep ~

"The universe offers you three things that
money cannot buy: joy, love, and life."

~ Matshona Dhliwayo

26 ▶ _____

_____

WHY I want to do this ~

_____

Things I **NEED** ~

_____

_____ DATE ACCOMPLISHED _____ _Ready, steady..._ ➤ _GO!!!_

My Experience ~ ☆ ☆ ☆ ☆ ☆

Awesome learnings & MEMORIES to keep ~

_____

_____

_____

_____

_____

_____

_____

_____

_____

_____

WHY I want to do this ~

Things I **NEED** ~

Ready, steady... **GO!!!** DATE ACCOMPLISHED

My Experience ~ ☆ ☆ ☆ ☆ ☆

Awesome learnings & MEMORIES to keep ~

"You must not lose faith in humanity. Humanity is an
ocean; if a few drops of the ocean are dirty,
the ocean does not become dirty."

~ Mahatma Gandhi

28 ▶ _____

_____

WHY I want to do this ~

Things I **NEED** ~

DATE ACCOMPLISHED — *Ready, steady...* ♂ *GO!!!*

My Experience ~ ☆☆☆☆☆

Awesome learnings & MEMORIES to keep ~

▶ _____

29

WHY I want to do this ~

_____

Things I **NEED** ~

_____

Ready, steady... ♂ *GO!!!* _____
DATE ACCOMPLISHED

My Experience ~ ☆ ☆ ☆ ☆ ☆

_____

Awesome learnings & MEMORIES to keep ~

_____
_____
_____
_____
_____
_____
_____
_____

"Our greatest glory is not in never failing,
but in rising every time we fall."

~ Confucius

30

_____

_____

WHY I want to do this ~

_____

Things I **NEED** ~

_____

DATE ACCOMPLISHED   _Ready, steady..._ ➙ _GO!!!_

My Experience ~ ☆ ☆ ☆ ☆ ☆

Awesome learnings & MEMORIES to keep ~

_____

_____

_____

_____

_____

_____

_____

_____

_____

_____

_____

_____

WHY I want to do this ~

_____

Things I **NEED** ~

_____

Ready, steady... ➤ *GO!!!* _____ DATE ACCOMPLISHED

My Experience ~ ☆ ☆ ☆ ☆ ☆

Awesome learnings & MEMORIES to keep ~

_____

_____

_____

_____

_____

_____

_____

"Life is like riding a bicycle. To keep your
balance, you must keep moving."

~ Albert Einstein

32

_____

_____

WHY I want to do this ~

Things I **NEED** ~

DATE ACCOMPLISHED   *Ready, steady...* ➤ *GO!!!*

My Experience ~ ☆ ☆ ☆ ☆ ☆

Awesome learnings & MEMORIES to keep ~

▶ _____

33

_____

WHY I want to do this ~
_____

Things I **NEED** ~
_____

Ready, steady... 🚀 *GO!!!* _____
DATE ACCOMPLISHED

My Experience ~ ☆ ☆ ☆ ☆ ☆

Awesome learnings & MEMORIES to keep ~

_____

_____

_____

_____

_____

_____

_____

_____

"You have been assigned this mountain so that
you can show others it can be moved."

~ Mel Robbins (The 5 Second Rule)

34

WHY I want to do this ~

Things I **NEED** ~

DATE ACCOMPLISHED   *Ready, steady...* **GO!!!**

My Experience ~ ☆ ☆ ☆ ☆ ☆

Awesome learnings & MEMORIES to keep ~

▶ _____

35

_____

WHY I want to do this ~
_____

Things I **NEED** ~
_____

Ready, steady... ➤ *GO!!!* _____
DATE ACCOMPLISHED

My Experience ~ ☆ ☆ ☆ ☆ ☆
_____

Awesome learnings & MEMORIES to keep ~
_____
_____
_____
_____
_____
_____
_____
_____

"Wherever you go, go with all your heart."

~ Confucius

36 ▶ _____

_____

WHY I want to do this ~

Things I **NEED** ~

————— DATE ACCOMPLISHED ————— *Ready, steady...* ➜ *GO!!!*

My Experience ~ ☆☆☆☆☆

Awesome learnings & MEMORIES to keep ~

WHY I want to do this ~

Things I **NEED** ~

Ready, steady... ➤ *GO!!!* DATE ACCOMPLISHED

My Experience ~ ☆ ☆ ☆ ☆ ☆

Awesome learnings & MEMORIES to keep ~

"All great achievements require time."

~ Maya Angelou

38 ▶ _____
_____

WHY I want to do this ~
_____
_____

Things I **NEED** ~
_____
_____

DATE ACCOMPLISHED — *Ready, steady...* **GO!!!**

My Experience ~ ☆ ☆ ☆ ☆ ☆
_____

Awesome learnings & MEMORIES to keep ~
_____
_____
_____
_____
_____
_____
_____
_____
_____
_____
_____

WHY I want to do this ~

Things I **NEED** ~

Ready, steady... ♂ *GO!!!* _____
DATE ACCOMPLISHED

My Experience ~ ☆ ☆ ☆ ☆ ☆

Awesome learnings & MEMORIES to keep ~

"The only difference between a rich person and
poor person is how they use their time."

~ Robert Kiyosaki

40

_____

_____

WHY I want to do this ~
_____

_____

Things I **NEED** ~
_____

_____

_____ DATE ACCOMPLISHED _____ *Ready, steady...* **GO!!!**

My Experience ~ ☆ ☆ ☆ ☆ ☆
_____

Awesome learnings & MEMORIES to keep ~
_____

_____

_____

_____

_____

_____

_____

_____

_____

_____

► _____

_____

WHY I want to do this ~

_____

Things I **NEED** ~

_____

Ready, steady... 🏹 *GO!!!* _____
DATE ACCOMPLISHED

My Experience ~ ☆ ☆ ☆ ☆ ☆

_____

Awesome learnings & MEMORIES to keep ~

_____

_____

_____

_____

_____

_____

_____

_____

_____

> "You must be the change you wish
> to see in the world."
>
> ~ Mahatma Gandhi

42

_____

_____

WHY I want to do this ~

_____

Things I **NEED** ~

_____

_____ Ready, steady... ➜ GO!!!
DATE ACCOMPLISHED

My Experience ~ ☆☆☆☆☆

Awesome learnings & MEMORIES to keep ~

_____

_____

_____

_____

_____

_____

_____

_____

_____

_____

▶ _____

43

_____

WHY I want to do this ~

Things I **NEED** ~

Ready, steady... ➤ *GO!!!* _____
DATE ACCOMPLISHED

My Experience ~ ☆ ☆ ☆ ☆ ☆

Awesome learnings & MEMORIES to keep ~

"Try not to become a man of success but rather
to become a man of value."

~ Albert Einstein

44 ▶ _____
_____

WHY I want to do this ~
_____

Things I **NEED** ~
_____

_____ DATE ACCOMPLISHED _____ *Ready, steady...* **GO!!!**

My Experience ~ ☆ ☆ ☆ ☆ ☆

Awesome learnings & MEMORIES to keep ~

▶ _____

45

_____

WHY I want to do this ~

Things I **NEED** ~

Ready, steady... ➤ *GO!!!* _____
DATE ACCOMPLISHED

My Experience ~ ☆ ☆ ☆ ☆ ☆

Awesome learnings & MEMORIES to keep ~

"The two most important days in your life are the day
you are born and the day you find out why."

~ Mark Twain

46 ▶ _____

_____

WHY I want to do this ~

_____

Things I **NEED** ~

_____

_____ *Ready, steady...* 🏃 *GO!!!*
DATE ACCOMPLISHED

My Experience ~ ☆☆☆☆☆

Awesome learnings & MEMORIES to keep ~

_____
_____
_____
_____
_____
_____
_____
_____
_____
_____

WHY I want to do this ~

Things I **NEED** ~

Ready, steady... ☞ *GO!!!*

My Experience ~ ☆ ☆ ☆ ☆ ☆

Awesome learnings & MEMORIES to keep ~

"The best way to find yourself is to lose yourself
in the service of others."

~ Mahatma Gandhi

48 ▶ _____

WHY I want to do this ~

Things I **NEED** ~

_____ *Ready, steady...* ➤ *GO!!!*
DATE ACCOMPLISHED

My Experience ~ ☆ ☆ ☆ ☆ ☆

Awesome learnings & MEMORIES to keep ~

▶ _____

49

WHY I want to do this ~

Things I **NEED** ~

Ready, steady... ♂ *GO!!!* _____
DATE ACCOMPLISHED

My Experience ~ ☆ ☆ ☆ ☆ ☆

Awesome learnings & MEMORIES to keep ~

"Do not let the behavior of others
destroy your inner peace."

~ Dalai Lama

50 ▶ _____
_____
_____

WHY I want to do this ~
_____
_____

Things I **NEED** ~
_____
_____

——— DATE ACCOMPLISHED ——— *Ready, steady...* ➔ *GO!!!*

My Experience ~ ☆ ☆ ☆ ☆ ☆
_____

Awesome learnings & MEMORIES to keep ~
_____
_____
_____
_____
_____
_____
_____
_____
_____
_____
_____

▶ _____

_____

WHY I want to do this ~

Things I **NEED** ~

Ready, steady... ➳ *GO!!!* _____
DATE ACCOMPLISHED

My Experience ~ ☆ ☆ ☆ ☆ ☆

Awesome learnings & MEMORIES to keep ~

"The nearer a man comes to a calm mind,
the closer he is to strength."

~ Marcus Aurelius

52 ▶ _____

_____

WHY I want to do this ~

Things I **NEED** ~

DATE ACCOMPLISHED — _Ready, steady..._ ➹ _GO!!!_

My Experience ~ ☆☆☆☆☆

Awesome learnings & MEMORIES to keep ~

▶

53

WHY I want to do this ~

Things I **NEED** ~

Ready, steady... ♂ *GO!!!* _____
DATE ACCOMPLISHED

My Experience ~ ☆ ☆ ☆ ☆ ☆

Awesome learnings & MEMORIES to keep ~

"Well done is better than well said."

~ Benjamin Franklin

54 ▶ _____

_____

WHY I want to do this ~

Things I **NEED** ~

My Experience ~ ☆ ☆ ☆ ☆ ☆

Awesome learnings & MEMORIES to keep ~

WHY I want to do this ~

Things I **NEED** ~

Ready, steady... 🚀 *GO!!!* _____ DATE ACCOMPLISHED

My Experience ~ ☆ ☆ ☆ ☆ ☆

Awesome learnings & MEMORIES to keep ~

"Trade your expectation for appreciation
and the world changes instantly."

~ Tony Robbins

56 ▶ _____

_____

WHY I want to do this ~

_____

Things I **NEED** ~

_____

_____ DATE ACCOMPLISHED   *Ready, steady...* ✗ *GO!!!*

My Experience ~ ☆ ☆ ☆ ☆ ☆

Awesome learnings & MEMORIES to keep ~

_____

_____

_____

_____

_____

_____

_____

_____

_____

▶ _____

_____

WHY I want to do this ~

_____

Things I **NEED** ~

_____

Ready, steady... ✪➔ *GO!!!* _____ DATE ACCOMPLISHED

My Experience ~ ☆ ☆ ☆ ☆ ☆

_____

Awesome learnings & MEMORIES to keep ~

_____

_____

_____

_____

_____

_____

_____

_____

"Life is not a problem to be solved
but a reality to be experienced."

~ Soren Kierkegaard

58

_____

WHY I want to do this ~

Things I **NEED** ~

DATE ACCOMPLISHED

Ready, steady... **GO!!!**

My Experience ~ ☆☆☆☆☆

Awesome learnings & MEMORIES to keep ~

▶ _____

_____

WHY I want to do this ~

Things I **NEED** ~

Ready, steady... ➤ *GO!!!* _____
DATE ACCOMPLISHED

My Experience ~ ☆ ☆ ☆ ☆ ☆

Awesome learnings & MEMORIES to keep ~

"Breathe. Let go. And remind yourself that this very moment is the only one you know you have for sure."

~ Oprah Winfrey

60 ▶ _____
_____

WHY I want to do this ~
_____

Things I **NEED** ~
_____

DATE ACCOMPLISHED   *Ready, steady...* ♂ *GO!!!*

My Experience ~ ☆☆☆☆☆

Awesome learnings & MEMORIES to keep ~
_____
_____
_____
_____
_____
_____
_____
_____
_____
_____

▶ _____

61

_____

WHY I want to do this ~
_____

Things I **NEED** ~
_____

Ready, steady... ➡ GO!!! _____
DATE ACCOMPLISHED

My Experience ~ ☆ ☆ ☆ ☆ ☆
_____

Awesome learnings & MEMORIES to keep ~
_____
_____
_____
_____
_____
_____
_____
_____

"Life is really simple, but men insist
on making it complicated."

~ Confucius

62 ▶ _____
_____

WHY I want to do this ~ _____
_____

Things I **NEED** ~ _____
_____

DATE ACCOMPLISHED _____ *Ready, steady...* ➤ *GO!!!*

My Experience ~ ☆☆☆☆☆

Awesome learnings & MEMORIES to keep ~
_____
_____
_____
_____
_____
_____
_____
_____
_____
_____
_____

WHY I want to do this ~

Things I **NEED** ~

Ready, steady... ♂ *GO!!!* _____
DATE ACCOMPLISHED

My Experience ~ ☆ ☆ ☆ ☆ ☆

Awesome learnings & MEMORIES to keep ~

"The secret of happiness, you see, is not found in seeking
more, but in developing the capacity to enjoy less."

~ S o c r a t e s

64 ▶ _____

_____

WHY I want to do this ~
_____

Things I **NEED** ~
_____

_____ DATE ACCOMPLISHED _____ *Ready, steady...* ♂ *GO!!!*

My Experience ~ ☆ ☆ ☆ ☆ ☆

Awesome learnings & MEMORIES to keep ~
_____
_____
_____
_____
_____
_____
_____
_____
_____
_____

▶ _____

_____

65

_____

WHY I want to do this ~

_____

Things I **NEED** ~

_____

Ready, steady... ✏️ **GO!!!** _____
DATE ACCOMPLISHED

My Experience ~ ☆ ☆ ☆ ☆ ☆

Awesome learnings & MEMORIES to keep ~

_____

_____

_____

_____

_____

_____

_____

_____

"Dwell on the beauty of life. Watch the
stars, and see yourself running with them."

~ Marcus Aurelius

66 ▶ _____

_____

WHY I want to do this ~
_____

Things I **NEED** ~
_____

_____ **DATE ACCOMPLISHED** _____ *Ready, steady...* 🡒 *GO!!!*

My Experience ~ ☆ ☆ ☆ ☆ ☆

Awesome learnings & MEMORIES to keep ~
_____

_____

_____

_____

_____

_____

_____

_____

_____

_____

▶ _____

67

_____

WHY I want to do this ~

Things I **NEED** ~

Ready, steady... 🏹 *GO!!!* _____
DATE ACCOMPLISHED

My Experience ~ ☆ ☆ ☆ ☆ ☆

Awesome learnings & MEMORIES to keep ~

"Love yourself first and everything falls into line."

~ Lucille Ball

68

WHY I want to do this ~

Things I **NEED** ~

DATE ACCOMPLISHED — Ready, steady... GO!!!

My Experience ~ ☆☆☆☆☆

Awesome learnings & MEMORIES to keep ~

▶ _____

69

_____

WHY I want to do this ~

Things I **NEED** ~

Ready, steady... ♂ *GO!!!* _____
DATE ACCOMPLISHED

My Experience ~ ☆ ☆ ☆ ☆ ☆

Awesome learnings & MEMORIES to keep ~

_____

_____

_____

_____

_____

_____

_____

_____

_____

"Hoping drains your energy. Action creates energy."

~ Robert Kiyosaki

70

▶ _____

WHY I want to do this ~

Things I **NEED** ~

_____ DATE ACCOMPLISHED _____ *Ready, steady...* ➤ *GO!!!*

My Experience ~ ☆ ☆ ☆ ☆ ☆

Awesome learnings & MEMORIES to keep ~

▶ _____

71

_____

WHY I want to do this ~
_____

Things I **NEED** ~
_____

Ready, steady... 🔫 *GO!!!* _____
DATE ACCOMPLISHED

My Experience ~ ☆ ☆ ☆ ☆ ☆
_____

Awesome learnings & MEMORIES to keep ~
_____
_____
_____
_____
_____
_____
_____
_____

"In dreams and in love there are no impossibilities."

~ Janos Arany

72

WHY I want to do this ~

Things I **NEED** ~

DATE ACCOMPLISHED

Ready, steady... GO!!!

My Experience ~ ☆ ☆ ☆ ☆ ☆

Awesome learnings & MEMORIES to keep ~

▶ _____

WHY I want to do this ~

Things I **NEED** ~

Ready, steady... 🏃 **GO!!!** _____
DATE ACCOMPLISHED

My Experience ~ ☆ ☆ ☆ ☆ ☆

Awesome learnings & MEMORIES to keep ~

"When you realize how perfect everything is you will
tilt your head back and laugh at the sky."

~ Buddha

74 ▶ _____

WHY I want to do this ~ _____

Things I **NEED** ~ _____

DATE ACCOMPLISHED   *Ready, steady...* ➤ *GO!!!*

My Experience ~ ☆☆☆☆☆

Awesome learnings & MEMORIES to keep ~

75

_____

_____

WHY I want to do this ~

Things I **NEED** ~

Ready, steady... 🏹 *GO!!!* _____

DATE ACCOMPLISHED

My Experience ~ ☆ ☆ ☆ ☆ ☆

Awesome learnings & MEMORIES to keep ~

"Of all days, the day on which one has not
laughed is the one most surely wasted."

~ Sebastien Roch

76

▶ _____
_____

WHY I want to do this ~
_____

Things I **NEED** ~ ·
_____

My Experience ~ ☆ ☆ ☆ ☆ ☆
_____

Awesome learnings & MEMORIES to keep ~
_____
_____
_____
_____
_____
_____
_____
_____
_____
_____
_____

▶ _____

_____

WHY I want to do this ~

Things I **NEED** ~

Ready, steady... ➤ *GO!!!* _____
DATE ACCOMPLISHED

My Experience ~ ☆ ☆ ☆ ☆ ☆

Awesome learnings & MEMORIES to keep ~

"Your life is an expression of
all your thoughts."

~ Marcus Aurelius

78

WHY I want to do this ~

Things I **NEED** ~

DATE ACCOMPLISHED — *Ready, steady...* GO!!!

My Experience ~ ☆☆☆☆☆

Awesome learnings & MEMORIES to keep ~

_____

WHY I want to do this ~

Things I NEED ~

Ready, steady... ♂ *GO!!!* _____
DATE ACCOMPLISHED

My Experience ~ ☆ ☆ ☆ ☆ ☆

Awesome learnings & MEMORIES to keep ~

"Always believe that something wonderful
is about to happen."

~ S. S. Dhillon

80

_____

_____

WHY I want to do this ~

Things I **NEED** ~

DATE ACCOMPLISHED   *Ready, steady...* *GO!!!*

My Experience ~ ☆ ☆ ☆ ☆ ☆

Awesome learnings & MEMORIES to keep ~

▶ _____

81

_____

WHY I want to do this ~

Things I **NEED** ~

Ready, steady... ➤ *GO!!!* _____
DATE ACCOMPLISHED

My Experience ~ ☆ ☆ ☆ ☆ ☆

Awesome learnings & MEMORIES to keep ~

"You must find the place inside yourself
where nothing is impossible."

~ Deepak Chopra

82

_____
_____

WHY I want to do this ~
_____

Things I **NEED** ~
_____

_____ Ready, steady... GO!!!
DATE ACCOMPLISHED

My Experience ~ ☆ ☆ ☆ ☆ ☆
_____

Awesome learnings & MEMORIES to keep ~
_____
_____
_____
_____
_____
_____
_____
_____
_____
_____
_____

▶ _____

83

_____

WHY I want to do this ~

Things I **NEED** ~

Ready, steady... ➳ *GO!!!* _____
DATE ACCOMPLISHED

My Experience ~ ☆ ☆ ☆ ☆ ☆

Awesome learnings & MEMORIES to keep ~

"Nature is painting for us, day after day,
pictures of infinite beauty.

~ John Ruskin

84 ▶ _____

_____

WHY I want to do this ~
_____

Things I **NEED** ~
_____

_____ DATE ACCOMPLISHED _____ *Ready, steady...* ➤ *GO!!!*

My Experience ~ ☆ ☆ ☆ ☆ ☆

Awesome learnings & MEMORIES to keep ~

▶ _____

85

_____

WHY I want to do this ~

_____

Things I **NEED** ~

_____

Ready, steady... ✈ *GO!!!* _____
DATE ACCOMPLISHED

My Experience ~ ☆ ☆ ☆ ☆ ☆

_____

Awesome learnings & MEMORIES to keep ~

_____

_____

_____

_____

_____

_____

_____

_____

_____

"Always be on the lookout for
the presence of wonder."

~ E.B. White

86

WHY I want to do this ~

Things I **NEED** ~

DATE ACCOMPLISHED — Ready, steady... GO!!!

My Experience ~ ☆ ☆ ☆ ☆ ☆

Awesome learnings & MEMORIES to keep ~

▶ _____

87

_____

WHY I want to do this ~

Things I **NEED** ~

Ready, steady... 🏹 *GO!!!* _____
DATE ACCOMPLISHED

My Experience ~ ☆ ☆ ☆ ☆ ☆

Awesome learnings & MEMORIES to keep ~

"The quieter you become,
the more you are able to hear."

~ Rumi

88

WHY I want to do this ~

Things I **NEED** ~

DATE ACCOMPLISHED — *Ready, steady...* **GO!!!**

My Experience ~ ☆☆☆☆☆

Awesome learnings & MEMORIES to keep ~

WHY I want to do this ~

Things I **NEED** ~

Ready, steady... **GO!!!** _____ DATE ACCOMPLISHED

My Experience ~ ☆ ☆ ☆ ☆ ☆

Awesome learnings & MEMORIES to keep ~

"The simple things are also the most extraordinary things, and only the wise can see them."

~ Paulo Coelho

90

WHY I want to do this ~

Things I **NEED** ~

DATE ACCOMPLISHED   *Ready, steady...* *GO!!!*

My Experience ~ ☆☆☆☆☆

Awesome learnings & MEMORIES to keep ~

▶ _____

91

WHY I want to do this ~

Things I **NEED** ~

Ready, steady... 🏃 *GO!!!* _____

My Experience ~ ☆ ☆ ☆ ☆ ☆

Awesome learnings & MEMORIES to keep ~

"Sometimes it takes only one act of kindness and caring to change a person's life."

~ Jackie Chan

92

_____
_____

WHY I want to do this ~
_____

Things I **NEED** ~
_____

DATE ACCOMPLISHED — _Ready, steady..._ **GO!!!**

My Experience ~ ☆ ☆ ☆ ☆ ☆

Awesome learnings & MEMORIES to keep ~
_____
_____
_____
_____
_____
_____
_____
_____
_____
_____

▶ _____

_____ **93**

WHY I want to do this ~

Things I **NEED** ~

Ready, steady... ➤ *GO!!!* _____
DATE ACCOMPLISHED

My Experience ~ ☆ ☆ ☆ ☆ ☆

Awesome learnings & MEMORIES to keep ~

"If you judge people, you have
no time to love them."

~ Mother Teresa

94 ▶ _____

_____

WHY I want to do this ~

Things I **NEED** ~

DATE ACCOMPLISHED — _Ready, steady..._ ➤ _GO!!!_

My Experience ~ ☆ ☆ ☆ ☆ ☆

Awesome learnings & MEMORIES to keep ~

WHY I want to do this ~

Things I **NEED** ~

Ready, steady... **GO!!!** _____
DATE ACCOMPLISHED

My Experience ~ ☆ ☆ ☆ ☆ ☆

Awesome learnings & MEMORIES to keep ~

"Patience is the most beautiful prayer."

~ Indian Proverb

_____

WHY I want to do this ~

Things I **NEED** ~

 Ready, steady... GO!!!

DATE ACCOMPLISHED

My Experience ~ ☆ ☆ ☆ ☆ ☆

Awesome learnings & MEMORIES to keep ~

_____

_____

WHY I want to do this ~

_____

Things I **NEED** ~

_____

Ready, steady... ➤ *GO!!!* _____
DATE ACCOMPLISHED

My Experience ~ ☆ ☆ ☆ ☆ ☆

_____

Awesome learnings & MEMORIES to keep ~

_____

_____

_____

_____

_____

_____

_____

"Do what you can, with what you have,
where you are."

~ Theodore Roosevelt

98

WHY I want to do this ~

Things I **NEED** ~

DATE ACCOMPLISHED   *Ready, steady...* GO!!!

My Experience ~ ☆☆☆☆☆

Awesome learnings & MEMORIES to keep ~

▶ _____

99

_____

WHY I want to do this ~
_____

Things I **NEED** ~
_____

Ready, steady... 🏹 *GO!!!* _____
DATE ACCOMPLISHED

My Experience ~ ☆ ☆ ☆ ☆ ☆

Awesome learnings & MEMORIES to keep ~

_____
_____
_____
_____
_____
_____
_____
_____

"Life is not the amount of breaths you take, it's the
moments that take your breath away."

~ Bob Moorehead

100 ▶ _____

_____

WHY I want to do this ~

_____

Things I **NEED** ~

_____

_____ DATE ACCOMPLISHED _____ _Ready, steady..._ ➹ _GO!!!_

My Experience ~ ☆ ☆ ☆ ☆ ☆

Awesome learnings & MEMORIES to keep ~

_____

_____

_____

_____

_____

_____

_____

_____

_____

_____

100 Extra Epic ideas to get you started...

"When we do something we like, we are not only happy, we are also very strong."

~ Rossana Condoleo

- CROSS 12 HANGING BRIDGES ON FOOT
- BURY A TIME CAPSULE AND DIG IT UP AFTER 8 YEARS
- LIVE IN A FARMHOUSE & TAKE CARE OF FARM ANIMALS FOR A WEEK
- HATCH A REAL EGG OR WATCH AN EGG HATCHING IN REAL LIFE
- WALK ON EGG SHELLS AND ENJOY THE CRUNCHY SOUND
- DO A WHOLE BODY MASSAGE USING COFFEE GROUNDS
- SNORKEL IN 10 PARADISE BEACHES WITH SOMEONE I LOVE
- PLANT 10 DIFFERENT KINDS OF VEGETABLES AND HERBS
- COOK A FISH ON A BONFIRE LIKE A SHIPWRECK SURVIVOR
- FIND THE ULTIMATE CURE TO STOP A PANDEMIC

- BUILD AN IRON MAN SUIT
- VISIT THE OLDEST LIBRARIES IN THE WORLD
- VOLUNTEER AT AN ANIMAL SHELTER OR ADOPT ONE
- ADVOCATE FOR A GOOD CAUSE AND BE PASSIONATE ABOUT IT
- BE A LIVE STUDIO AUDIENCE OR BE AN 'EXTRA' IN A HOLLYWOOD MOVIE
- PERFORM IN FRONT OF 1,000 PEOPLE... 6 TIMES
- VISIT 12 LIGHTHOUSES AND TAKE A SELFIE IN THE TOWER
- VISIT 10 CITIES IN ASIA BEFORE AGE ___
- GO NATURE TRIP ANYWHERE FOR A MONTH
- DO A WEEK LONG CROSS COUNTRY MOTORCYCLE RIDE

- WRITE A BOOK ABOUT MY CRAZY FAMILY
- TREAT MY FAMILY AND FRIENDS TO A CRUISE
- SLEEP IN A CASTLE FOR A DAY... WEARING A COSTUME
- DISCOVER A MEDICINAL PLANT THAT WILL CURE _____
- LEARN HOW TO INVEST AND FIND A WEALTHY MENTOR
- COLLECT ASSETS THAT APPRECIATES OVER TIME
- DIVE THE DEEPEST OCEAN IN FREESTYLE
- CLIMB THE HIGHEST PEAK IN FREESTYLE
- GIVE AWAY ALL MY CLOTHES (GO MINIMALIST!)
- START AN ONLINE GIG AND DO FREELANCE FOR FREE

- CREATE MY OWN ROBOT TO HELP ME DO HOUSEHOLD CHORES
- PLAY MONOPOLY FOR A MONTH AND BE FINANCIALLY SMART
- LEARN AN INCOME GENERATING HOBBY
- RECORD MY LAUGHTER AND PLAY IT WHENEVER I FEEL DOWN
- VISIT AN ANTIQUE SHOP AND BUY SOMETHING
- USE OLD THINGS - TYPEWRITER, CASSETTE PLAYER, DEEP WELL
- LEARN WOODWORK, ANIMAL HUSBUNDRY, & SURVIVAL SKILLS
- DRAW MY PORTRAIT... BLINDFOLDED
- WRITE A SONG OR A POEM AND DEDICATE IT TO SOMEONE
- WRITE A LETTER TO MY FUTURE SELF AND OPEN IT 10 YEARS LATER

- SAVE A LIFE
- PARAGLIDE IN SWITZERLAND
- GO OFF GRID FOR 10 DAYS (OR MORE)
- MEDITATE EVERY MORNING FOR 31 DAYS
- DRINK A HEALTHY SMOOTHIE FOR A YEAR OR A LIFETIME
- TEACH SOMEONE A SKILL / SHARE MY TALENTS
- TEACH A CHILD HOW TO READ, OR WRITE, OR RIDE A BIKE
- GROW MY HAIR LONG FOR A YEAR (OR LONGER)
- READ 100 BOOKS ABOUT MY FAVORITE SUBJECTS
- BINGE WATCH MY FAVORITE CHILDHOOD SHOWS AND MOVIES

- CELEBRATE ALL MY BIRTHDAYS BY THE BEACH
- LEARN TO SAY 'I LOVE YOU' IN 14 LANGUAGES
- BE PART OF AN OCEAN CLEAN UP GROUP
- SUPPORT PLASTIC FREE EARTH OR GO ZERO WASTE
- LEARN A SPORT AND WIN A MEDAL
- JOIN A DISASTER RELIEF PROGRAM OR ACTIVITY
- HUG PEOPLE I LOVE EVERYDAY FOR AS LONG AS I LIVE
- COMPLETE A 30-DAYS DAILY GRATITUDE HABIT
- GIVE A FREE MEAL TO A STRANGER IN NEED
- VISIT AN ORPHANAGE OR A RETIREMENT HOME

- RIDE A CAMEL, A HORSE, AND A CARABAO (IN THAT ORDER)
- OWN A RESTAURANT IN PARIS OR SOMEWHERE ROMANTIC
- ENJOY MULTIPLE STREAMS OF INCOME BY AGE _____
- ACHIEVE MY DREAM BODY (WEIGHT, SIZE, AND HEALTH)
- BLOW A THOUSAND BUBBLES WHILE DANCING IN THE RAIN
- CREATE A BEACH MURAL PAINTING IN MY ROOM OR THE BACKYARD
- RESTORE AN OLD FURNITURE / FAMILY HEIRLOOM
- BECOME A SELF PUBLISHED, BEST SELLING, AWARD WINNING AUTHOR
- HAVE TEN THOUSAND FOLLOWERS IN ONE SOCIAL MEDIA PLATFORM
- MAKE AN APP, LEARN TO CODE, BE A TECH EXPERT

- SOAK IN A HOT SPRING IN JAPAN AND EAT A BOWL OF RAMEN
- HAVE A CLUTTER FREE LIFE... FOREVER
- HAVE A GRAND SEAFOOD FEAST WITH MY FAMILY IN AN EXCLUSIVE ISLAND
- PICK GRAPES IN A VINEYARD AND BRING HOME A BOTTLE
- STAND UNDER A WATERFALL AND BE DRENCHED ALL THE WAY
- VISIT A CAVE (AND SLEEP THERE IF I AM BRAVE ENOUGH)
- TRAVEL FIRST CLASS FOR VACATION TO MEET A CELEBRITY
- RIDE IN A SUBMARINE
- ENJOY A HELICOPTER RIDE
- GO TO OUTER SPACE

- PHOTOGRAPH THE MOST BEAUTIFUL WOMAN IN THE WORLD
- LIST DOWN 10 SIMPLE PLEASURES THAT ARE TOTALLY FREE
- TRAP A HANDFUL OF CLOUD INSIDE A JAR
- SPEND THE NIGHT ONBOARD A TRAIN
- OWN A HOTEL IN A TOURIST DESTINATION
- WEAR A HUGE MASCOT COSTUME FOR A CHILDREN'S PARTY
- BECOME A JEDI KNIGHT OR OWN A LEGIT STAR WARS LIGHT SABER
- UPGRADE MY RELATIONSHIP SKILLS
- OWN A MILLION DOLLAR WORTH OF GOLD
- BELIEVE IN MIRACLES

- TOUCH A SUNKEN SHIP
- TOUCH AN ICEBERG BEFORE IT ALL DISAPPEARS
- MAKE SOMEONE'S DREAM COME TRUE... NO MATTER HOW SIMPLE
- SCOOP A SPOON OF DIRT FROM A SPECIAL PLACE AND KEEP IT IN A BOTTLE
- WRITE A BOOK OF JOKES AND SUPER FUNNY STORIES
- VISIT THE GRANDEST ARCHITECTURAL BUILDINGS IN THE WORLD
- CREATE A LAW THAT WILL END WORLD HUNGER
- BECOME A BILLIONAIRE
- TALK TO MY OLDEST RELATIVE AND COMPLETE OUR FAMILY TREE
- GROW OLD, WISE, WEALTHY, AND HAPPY

More helpful suggestions:

Go through this list a few times a month and highlight the ones that catches your eye, or underline the ones that makes you feel excited about.

Share some of these suggestions to your close friends and family, and see if you can do them together.

Enjoyed our book? Want to share your ideas?

Write us an email -- **paperpandapress@gmail.com**

You may also leave a comment/review on **Amazon.com** and let us know your thoughts. Cheers!

Manufactured by Amazon.ca
Bolton, ON

26581189R00067